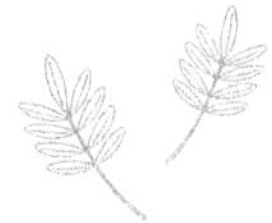
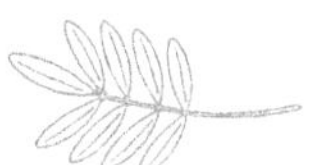
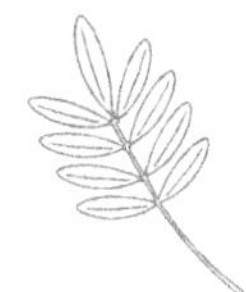

The Stories about Collecting happiness

NAME:

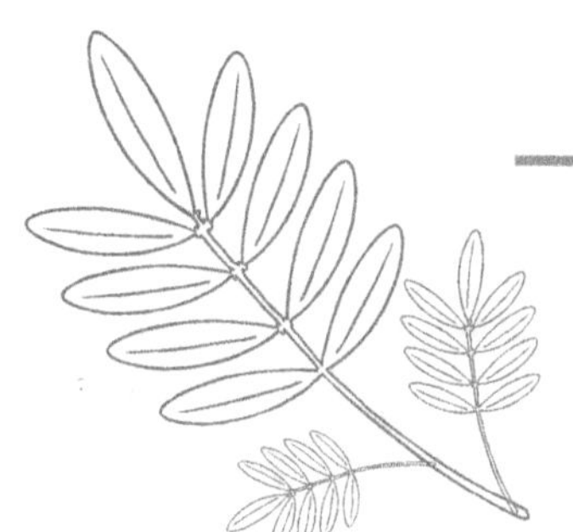
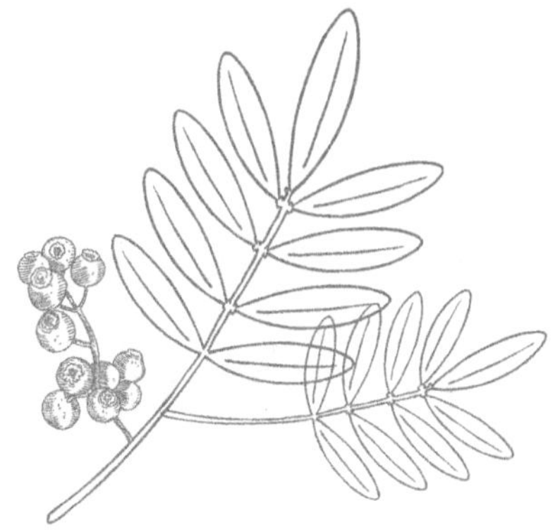

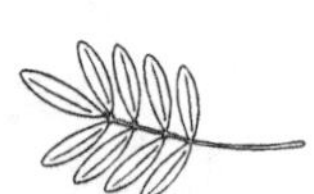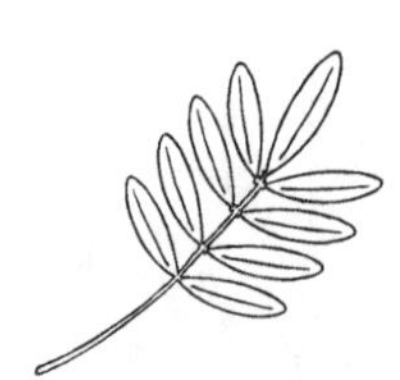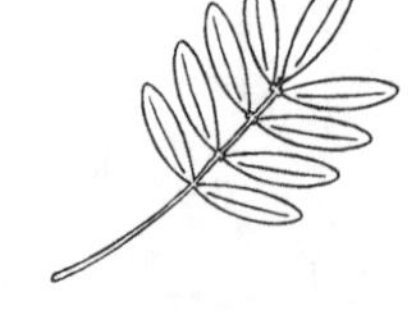

Happiness is a butterfly,

which when pursued is always just beyond your grasp,

but which if you sit down quietly,

may alight upon you.

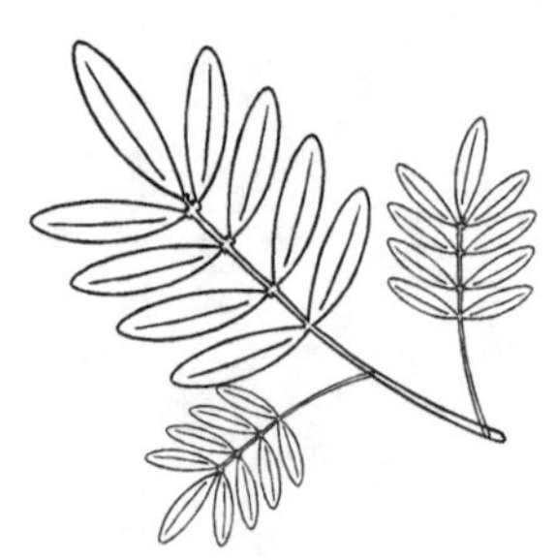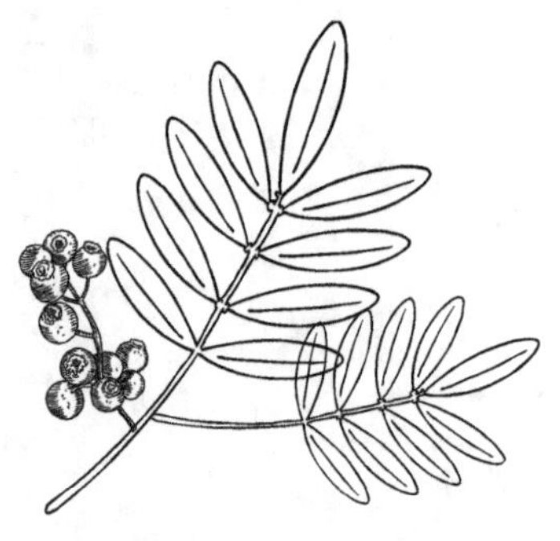